GW00471191

ACKNOWLEDGEMENT

The Judicial Services Board for Northern Ireland gratefully acknowledges the work done by the Committee in producing these guidelines. The members of the Committee were The Honourable Mr Justice McCollum, His Honour Judge Russell, His Honour Judge Smyth, His Honour Judge McKay, Mr E A Comerton QC, Mr T M Horner QC, Mr B J Stewart of O'Reilly Stewart, Solicitors and Mr G A Jones of C&H Jefferson, Solicitors, under the chairmanship of The Right Honourable. Lord Justice MacDermott.

The Board also acknowledges the assistance provided by the Judicial Studies Board for England and Wales ('JSB') in permitting the format and injury classifications in respect of these guidelines to be modelled on guidelines compiled for the JSB by Mr John Cherry QC, Mr Edwin Glasgow QC, Mr D A K Hughes, Solicitor, Mr R J Sutcliffe, Solicitor and His Honour Judge Roger Cox and published by Blackstone Press Limited.

CONTENTS

INTRODUCTION

by The Right Honourable Lord Justice MacDermott

This Committee was set up by the Lord Chief Justice at the suggestion of the Judicial Studies Board for Northern Ireland. In March 1992 the first edition of the *Guidelines for the Assessment of General Damages* was published in England and the Board felt that it would be helpful to Practitioners and others concerned with the assessment of damages if a Northern Ireland edition were produced.

Our initial approach to our task was to question the wisdom of such a venture. The assessment of damages is not an exact science: it is not a mechanical process achieved by recourse to an analysis of allegedly comparable cases or reference to well known books such as *Kemp and Kemp*. A fair assessment is achieved by the Judge applying his training, experience and innate sense of fairness to the individual case which he is trying and which he will approach both sensibly and with sensitivity. There is a real argument that "guidelines" will become "norms" and that the existence of a book of this nature will depersonalise the assessment of damages. On reflection, however, we concluded for several reasons that there should be a Northern Ireland Guidelines Book.

Firstly, the level of damages in Northern Ireland is significantly higher than in England and Wales. As was pointed out by Lord Lowry in *Simpson* v *Harland & Wolff* [1988] NI 432 this variation is in large measure due to the fact that in Northern Ireland the assessment of damages was in the hands of juries until 1987.

Secondly, Practitioners when valuing cases and Judges when assessing damages have had regard to the 1987 level of damages adjusted to reflect inflation.

Thirdly, if there are no local guidelines there is a danger that the existing English Guidelines will be accepted as relevant by default. This would be both irrational and unjust.

That said, we would emphasise that this book must be used with caution and discretion. It must not be considered as a "ready-reckoner" which by reference will provide an instant valuation to every case. The suggested valuations are guidelines and will best be used as a check upon a tentative valuation reached after a careful consideration of how particular injuries affect a particular individual.

A meaningful valuation of general damages depends upon many variables such as age, sex, pre-accident health and so on. The guidelines in this book are often given as a wide bracket so that these variable features may be fitted in and they are also wide so that they may last for a number of years without being rendered unreal by the erosion of inflation.

We have followed the headings adopted in the original book with some minor variations. They are, however, somewhat rigid and do not reflect the frequent situation where injuries are multiple and their sequelae varied and at times overlapping.

Finally, we would repeat what we have already said: this book must be used cautiously and sensibly. The figures which we suggest are no more than guidelines and must always be treated as such and kept under regular review.

25 octobre 1996

1. INJURIES INVOLVING PARALYSIS

(a) Quadriplegia   £250,000 - £400,000

Considerations affecting the level of the award:

(i) Extent of residual movement

(ii) Pain

(iii) Effect on other senses

(iv) Depression

(v) Age and life expectancy

(b) Paraplegia   £200,000 - £300,000

Considerations affecting the level of the award:

(i) Pain

(ii) Depression

(iii) Age and life expectancy

2. HEAD INJURIES

(a) Very Severe Brain Damage

£200,000 - £350,000

In the most severe cases the Plaintiff will be in a vegetative state; there may be recovery of eye opening and some return of sleep and waking rhythm and postural reflex movements; no evidence of meaningful response to environment. Unable to obey commands; no language functions and need for 24-hour nursing care.

Considerations affecting the level of the award:

(i) Insight

(ii) Life expectancy

(iii) Extent of physical limitations

(b) Moderately Severe Brain Damage

£150,000 - £300,000

Severe disability. Conscious, but total dependency and requiring constant care. Disabilities may be physical, eg limb paralysis, or cognitive, with marked impairment of intellect and personality.

Considerations affecting the level of the award:

(i) Insight

(ii) Life expectancy

(iii) Extent of physical limitations

(c) Moderate Brain Damage

(i) Moderate to severe intellectual deficit, a personality change, an effect on sight, speech and senses with an epileptic risk.	£150,000 - £250,000
(ii) Modest to moderate intellectual deficit, the ability to work is greatly reduced if not lost and there is a risk of epilepsy.	£75,000 - £150,000
(iii) Concentration and memory are affected, the ability to work is reduced and there may be a risk of epilepsy.	£25,000 - £100,000

(d) Minor Brain Damage   £25,000 - £50,000

A good recovery will have been made. The Plaintiff can participate in normal social life and return to work but restoration of all normal functions is not implicit. There may still be persistent defects such as poor concentration and memory or disinhibition of mood which may interfere with lifestyle, leisure activity and future work prospects.

Considerations affecting the level of the award:

(i) Extent and severity of the initial injury

(ii) Extent of any continuing and possibly permanent disability

(iii) Extent of any personality change

(e) Minor Head Injury   £2,000 - £20,000

These are not cases of brain damage from which they must be distinguished.

Considerations affecting the level of the award:

(i)   Severity of initial injury

(ii) Period of recovery from severe symptoms

(iii) Extent of continuing symptoms at trial

(iv) Headaches

(f) Established Epilepsy   £50,000 - £100,000

This includes both Grand mal and Petit mal.

The factors which will affect the award will be:

(i)   The existence of other associated behavioural problems.

(ii) Whether attacks are successfully controlled by medication and the extent to which the appreciation of the quality of life may be blunted by that medication.

3. PSYCHIATRIC DAMAGE

The factors to be taken into account in valuing claims for psychiatric damage include the following:

    (i)   Ability to cope with life and particularly work

    (ii)   Effect on relationships with family etc

    (iii)   Extent to which treatment would be successful

    (iv)   Future vulnerability

    (v)   Prognosis

    (vi)   The extent and/or nature of any associated physical injuries

    (vii)   Whether medical help has been sought.

A. Psychiatric Damage Generally

(a) Severe Psychiatric Damage	£30,000 - £100,000
(b) Moderately Severe Psychiatric Damage	£25,000 - £65,000
(c) Moderate Psychiatric Damage	£7,500 - £25,000
(d) Minor Psychiatric Damage	Up to £7,500

Considerations as to the level of the award will include the length of the period of disability and the ' extent to which daily activities were affected.

B. Post-traumatic Stress Disorder

An increasingly large number of cases deal with a specific reactive psychiatric disorder in which characteristic symptoms are displayed following a psychologically distressing event outside the range of human experience which would be markedly distressing to almost everyone.   Such symptoms would affect the basic functions such as breathing, pulse rate and bowel and/or bladder control.   They would also involve persistent re-experiencing of the relevant event, difficulty in controlling temper, in concentrating and in sleeping, and exaggerated startled response.

(a)   Severe   )
) £25,000 - £60,000
(b)   Moderately Severe   )

(c)   Moderate   £10,000 - £25,000

(d)   Minor   £2,500 - £7,500

4. INJURIES AFFECTING THE SENSES

Loss of or damage to senses can be restricted purely to one particular sense, eg loss of one eye or total blindness or loss of the sense of smell. However, very often damage to senses can be caused by other injuries. In such cases damages are likely to be viewed as "multiple injuries" awards.

A. Injuries affecting Sight

(a)	**Total Blindness and Deafness**	£200,000 - £300,000
(b)	**Total Blindness**	£150,000 - £250,000
(c)	**Total Loss of One Eye**	£40,000 - £75,000
(d)	**Loss of Sight in One Eye with Reduced Vision in the Remaining Eye**	
	(i) Where there is serious risk of further deterioration in the remaining eye, going beyond the normal risk of sympathetic ophthalmia.	£75,000 - £100,000
	(ii) Where there is reduced vision in the remaining eye and including any problems of eg double vision.	£50,000 - £100,000
(e)	**Complete Loss of Sight in One Eye**	£40,000 - £70,000
(f)	Cases of serious but incomplete loss of vision in one eye without significant risk of loss of or reduction in vision in the remaining eye, or where there is constant double vision.	£20,000 - £40,000

(g) Minor but permanent impairment of vision in one eye including cases where there is some double vision which may not be constant.	£10,000 - £25,000
(h) Minor Eye Injuries	Up to £10,000

B. Deafness

The word "deafness" is convenient to embrace total or partial hearing loss. However, in assessing awards for hearing loss regard must be had to the following:

(i) Whether the injury complained of is:

    (a)   A hearing impairment

    (b)   A disability

    (c)   A handicap

(ii) Whether the injury is one that has an immediate effect of causing one or more of the disabilities above or whether the same occurred over a period of time, eg in noise exposure cases.

(iii) Whether the injury/disability is one that the Plaintiff has suffered at an early age with the result that the same has had an effect upon his speech or if it is one that he has suffered in later life.

(a) Total Deafness and Loss of Speech	£150,000 - £250,000
(b) Total Deafness	£50,000 - £125,000
(c) Total Loss of Hearing in One Ear	£20,000 - £35,000

(d) Partial Hearing Loss/Tinnitus

(i)	Severe tinnitus	£20,000 - £30,000
(ii)	Moderate tinnitus and hearing loss	£10,000 - £20,000
(iii)	Mild tinnitus with some hearing loss	)
(iv)	Slight or occasional mild tinnitus with slight hearing loss	) Up to £10,000)

C. Impairment of Taste and Smell

(a)	**Total Loss of Taste and Smell**	)
(b)	**Total Loss of Smell and Significant Loss of Taste**	) £15,000 - £30,000)
(c)	**Loss of Smell**	£15,000 - £25,000
(d)	**Loss of Taste**	£10,000 - £20,000

5. INJURIES TO INTERNAL ORGANS

A. Chest Injuries

This is a specially difficult area because the vast majority of cases relate to industrial *disease* as distinct from traumatic *injury* and the level of the appropriate award for lung disease necessarily reflects the prognosis for the future and/or the risks of development of secondary sequelae (such as mesothelioma).

(a) Injuries leading to collapsed lungs from which a full and uncomplicated recovery is made.	£2,000 - £6,000
(b) Smoke inhalation which often leaves some residual damage which is not serious enough permanently to interfere with lung function.	£2,500 - £15,000
(c) Any <u>injury</u> affecting lung function and permanent damage to tissue.	£10,000 - £25,000
(d) Very worst cases of total removal of one lung with considerable and prolonged pain and suffering and permanent serious scarring will be in the region of the maximum award for chest injuries.	£50,000 - £75,000

B. Lung Disease

(a) Calcified plaques with pleural thickening but no present risk of functional impairment or of cancer.	£5,000 - £10,000
(b) Asbestosis (with the cancer risk left for a future award).	£15,000 - £25,000

(c)	Serious asbestosis cases.	£25,000 - £50,000
(d)	Cases with seriously disabling consequences and inevitable loss of life expectancy.	£50,000 - £75,000
(e)	Cases where death within a few years of trial is inevitable.	£50,000 - £100,000
(f)	Young Plaintiff where there is probability of progressive worsening leading to premature death.	£75,000 - £150,000

C. Digestive System

It is to be noted that the risk of associated damage to the reproductive organs is frequently encountered in cases of this nature and requires separate consideration.

(a)	Penetrating stab wounds or industrial laceration or serious seat-belt pressure cases.	£3,000 - £15,000
(b)	Serious damage with continuing pain or discomfort.	£20,000 - £50,000

D. Reproductive System

Male

(a)	Total impotence and loss of sexual function in the case of a young man.	£60,000 - £80,000

Cases at the very serious level will frequently involve incontinence or similar difficulties and will often be accompanied by psychological aggravation.

(b) <u>Sterility</u> - The more serious cases are those involving traumatic injury aggravated by scarring.   £50,000 - £75,000

(c) An uncomplicated case of infertility without any aggravating features for a young man without children.   £25,000 - £50,000

(d) Similar situation but involving a family man who might intend to have more children.   £15,000 - £35,000

(e) Cases where the infertility amounts to little more than an `insult'.   Up to £10,000

Female

(a) Infertility with associated depression and some anxiety and some pain and scarring.   £60,000 - £90,000

(b) Sterility without any complication and where the Plaintiff already has children.   £20,000 - £50,000

Where there are no complications and the Plaintiff already has children the award will be at the lower end of the bracket. The situation is, however, almost always complicated by significant psychological damage which will take it to the upper end of the bracket.

(c) Sterility where the Plaintiff would not have had children in any event (for example, because of age).   £5,000 - £15,000

(d) Failed sterilisation leading to unwanted pregnancy.   £15,000 - £20,000

E. Kidney

   (a) Loss of kidney with no damage to the other.

          £20,000 - £30,000

   (b) Where there is significant risk of future urinary tract infection or other total loss of natural kidney function. Such cases will invariably carry with them substantial future medical expenses which, in this field, are particulary high.

          £40,000 - £60,000

   (c) Serious and permanent damage to or loss of both kidneys.

          £75,000 - £100,000

F. Bowels

   (a) Total loss of natural function and dependence on colostomy, depending on age.

          £75,000 - £100,000

   (b) Impaired function with continuing problems and accidents and embarrassment.

          £30,000 - £50,000

   (c) Penetrating injuries causing some permanent damage but an eventual return to natural function control.

          £10,000 - £25,000

G. Bladder

   (a) Complete loss of natural function and control.

          £50,000 - £75,000

   (b) Impairment of control with some pain and incontinence.

          £25,000 - £50,000

   (c) Where there has been an almost complete recovery but some fairly long-term interference with natural function.

          £10,000 - £20,000

The cancer risk cases still occupy a special category and can properly attract awards at the top of the range even where natural function continues for the time being. Once the prognosis is firm and reliable the award must reflect the loss of life expectancy, the level of continuing pain and suffering and most significantly the extent to which the Plaintiff has to live with the knowledge of the consequences which his death will have for others.

H. Spleen

Present medical opinion suggests that this organ is more important throughout life than was previously thought.

Loss of spleen where there is a continuing risk of internal infection and disorders due to the damage to the immune system.   £17,500 - £25,000

I. Hernia

(a) Uncomplicated inguinal hernia with no other associated abdominal injury or damage.   £2,500 - £7,500

(b) Continuing pain and/or limitations on physical activities, sport or employment.   £7,500 - £15,000

6. ORTHOPAEDIC INJURIES

A. Neck Injuries

(a) Neck injury associated with incomplete paraplegia or resulting in permanent spastic quadriparesis or where despite the wearing of a collar 24 hours a day for a period of years, the neck could still not move and severe headaches have proved intractable.   £75,000 - £200,000

(b) Injury falling short of the disability in (a) above but being of considerable severity, eg permanent damage to the brachial plexus.   £50,000 - £100,000

(c) The injury is such as to cause severe damage to soft tissues and/or ruptured tendons and results in significant disability of a permanent nature.   £25,000 - £75,000

(d) Injuries and fractures or dislocation causing severe immediate symptoms or necessitating spinal fusion leaving significantly impaired function or vulnerability to further trauma, pain and limitation of activities.   £25,000 - £50,000

(e) Whiplash or wrenching-type injury and disc lesion of the more severe type, which may result in cervical spondylosis, serious limitation of movement, permanent or recurring pain, stiffness or discomfort, the potential need for further surgery or increased vulnerability to trauma.   £15,000 - £30,000

(f)	Relatively minor injuries which may or may not have exacerbated or accelerated some pre-existing unrelated condition but with, in any event, a complete recovery within a few years. This bracket will also apply to moderate whiplash injuries where the period of recovery is fairly protracted and where there is an increased vulnerability to further trauma.	£7,500 - £15,000
(g)	Minor soft tissue and whiplash injuries and the like where symptoms are moderate and full recovery takes place within, at most, two years.	Up to £7,500

B. Back Injuries

(a)	The most severe of back injuries which fall short of paralysis but the results of which include, for example, impotence.	£75,000 - £150,000
(b)	Special features exist which take the particular injury outside any lower bracket applicable to orthopaedic damage to the back, eg impaired bladder and bowel function, severe sexual difficulties and unsightly scarring.	£35,000 - £75,000
(c)	Serious back injury, involving disc lesions or fractures of discs or vertebral bodies where, despite treatment, there remains continuing pain or discomfort, impaired agility and sexual function, depression, personality change, alcoholism, unemployability and the risk of arthritis.	£30,000 - £60,000
(d)	Permanent residual disability albeit of less severity than in the higher bracket.	£15,000 - £30,000

This bracket contains a large number of different types of injury; eg a crush fracture of the lumbar vertebrae with risk of osteoarthritis and constant pain and discomfort and impaired sexual function, or traumatic spondylolisthesis with continuous pain and likelihood of spinal fusion, or prolapsed intervertebral disc with substantial acceleration of back degeneration.

(e) Moderate Back Injuries	£10,000 - £25,000

A wide variety of injuries qualify for inclusion within this bracket.   The precise figure depends upon the severity of the original injury and/or the existence of some permanent or chronic disability.

(f) Minor Back Injuries	Up to £10,000

For example, strains, sprains and disc prolapses and soft tissue injuries which have made a full recovery or resulted only in minor continuing disability or which have accelerated or exacerbated pre-existing unrelated conditions for a fairly brief period of time.

C. Injuries to Pelvis and Hips

(a) Extensive fractures of the pelvis involving, for example, dislocation of a lower back joint and a ruptured bladder or a hip injury resulting in spondylolisthesis of a low back joint with intolerable pain necessitating spinal fusion. Substantial residual disabilities, such as a complicated arthrodesis with residual lack of bowel and bladder control, sexual dysfunction or hip

deformity necessitating the use of a calliper, will be inevitable.	£60,000 - £100,000

(b) Injuries only a little less serious but with particular distinguishing features taking them out of any lower bracket. — £40,000 - £75,000

(c) Serious Injury to the Hip or Pelvis — £25,000 - £50,000

A variety of injuries fall within this bracket, such as a fracture of the acetabulum leading to degenerative changes and leg instability requiring an osteotomy and the likelihood of hip replacement surgery in the years ahead; or the fracture of an arthritic femur or hip necessitating the insertion of a hip joint; or a fracture resulting in hip replacement surgery being only partially successful with a clear risk of a need for revision surgery.

(d) Significant injury to the pelvis or hip but where any permanent disability is not major nor any future risk great. — £15,000 - £40,000

(e) Relatively minor hip or pelvic injuries with no residual disability. — Up to £15,000

D. Amputation of Arms

(a) Loss of Both Arms - The high figure would normally apply where the arms are lost at the shoulder region. — £150,000 - £300,000

(b) Loss of One Arm

The value of a lost arm depends upon:

(i)   Whether it is amputated below or above the elbow. The loss of the additional joint obviously adds greatly to the disability.

(ii)   Whether or not the amputation was of the dominant arm.

(iii)   The intensity of any phantom pains.

(1) *Arm amputated at the shoulder*	£75,000 - £100,000
(2) *Above elbow amputation*	£60,000 - £80,000

A shorter stump may create difficulties in the successful use of a prosthesis. This will make the level of the award towards the top end of the bracket. Amputation through the elbow however will normally produce an award at the lower end of the bracket.

(3) *Below elbow amputation*	£50,000 - £75,000

Amputation through the forearm with residual severe organic and phantom pains would attract an award at the upper end of the bracket.

E. Other Arm Injuries

(a) **Severe Injuries**	£40,000 - £75,000

Injuries which in terms of their severity fall short of amputation but which are extremely serious in their own right and leave the Plaintiff little better off than if he had lost his arm.

(b) **Injuries Resulting in Permanent and Substantial Disablement**	£25,000 - £40,000

Examples are serious fractures of one or both forearms where there is significant permanent residual disability whether functional or cosmetic.

(c) Less Severe Injury	£10,000 - £25,000

While there will have been significant disabilities, a substantial degree of recovery will have taken place or will be anticipated.

(d) Simple Fractures of the Forearm	Up to £10,000

F. Shoulder Injuries

(a) Serious Injury	£10,000 - £25,000

Dislocation of the shoulder and damage to the lower part of the brachial plexus causing pain in shoulder and neck, aching in elbow, sensory symptoms with forearm and hand and weakness of grip.

(b) Moderate Injury	£5,000 - £15,000

Frozen shoulder with limitation of movement and discomfort with symptoms persisting for some years.

(c) Minor Injury	Up to £7,500

Soft tissue injury to shoulder with considerable pain but almost complete recovery in less than one year.

G. Injuries to the Elbow

(a) A Severely Disabling Injury	£20,000 - £40,000
(b) Less Severe Injuries	£10,000 - £20,000

These injuries lead to impairment of function but do not involve major surgery or significant disability.

(c) Moderate or Minor Injury   Up to £10,000

Most elbow injuries fall into this category. They comprise a simple fracture, tennis elbow syndrome and lacerations; ie those injuries which cause no permanent damage and do not result in any permanent impairment of function.

H. Wrist Injuries

(a) Injuries resulting in complete loss of function in the wrist.   £20,000 - £40,000

(b) Injury resulting in significant permanent residual disability.   £15,000 - £30,000

(c) Less severe but still permanent disability as, for example, persisting pain and stiffness.   £10,000 - £25,000

(d) Where recovery is complete.   Up to £10,000

I. Hand Injuries

Of the arm, the hand is both functionally and cosmetically the most important feature. The loss of a hand is valued not far short of the amount which would be awarded for loss of an arm. The upper end of any bracket will generally be appropriate where the material injury is to the dominant hand.

(a) Total Effective Loss of Both Hands   £100,000 - £150,000

Serious injury resulting in extensive damage to both hands.

(b) Serious damage to both hands giving rise to permanent cosmetic disability and significant loss of function.

£50,000 - £100,000

(c) Total or Effective Loss of One Hand

£40,000 - £75,000

This bracket will apply to a hand which was crushed or thereafter surgically amputated or where all fingers and most of the palm have been traumatically amputated.   The upper end of the bracket is indicated where the hand so damaged was the dominant one.

(d) Amputation of index, middle and/or ring fingers, rendering hand of very little use with exceedingly weak grip.

£30,000 - £60,000

(e) Serious Hand Injuries

£30,000 - £60,000

For example, loss reducing hand to 50% capacity with, eg several fingers amputated and rejoined to hand leaving it clawed, clumsy and unsightly or amputation of some fingers together with part of the palm resulting in gross diminution of grip and dexterity and gross cosmetic disfigurement.

(f) Severe fractures to fingers with partial amputations and resulting in deformity, impairment of grip, reduced mechanical function and disturbed sensation.

£20,000 - £40,000

(g) Total Loss of Index Finger

£15,000 - £20,000

(h) Partial loss of index finger or injury giving rise to disfigurement and impairment of grip or dexterity.

£10,000 - £15,000

(i) Fracture of Index Finger

Up to £7,500

This level is appropriate where a fracture had mended quickly but grip has remained impaired, there is pain on heavy use and osteoarthritis is likely in due course.

(j)	**Total Loss of Middle Finger**	£10,000 - £15,000
(k)	**Serious Injury to Ring or Middle Fingers**	£7,500 - £15,000
(l)	Loss of terminal phalanx of the ring or middle fingers.	£5,000 - £10,000
(m)	Amputation of little finger	£7,500 - £15,000
(n)	Loss of part of the little finger where the remaining tip is unusually sensitive.	£5,000 - £7,500
(o)	**Amputation of Ring and Little Fingers**	£15,000 - £25,000
(p)	Amputation of the terminal phalanges of the index and middle fingers with further injury to the fourth finger, scarring and restriction of movement with grip and fine handling impaired.	£10,000 - £20,000
(q)	Fracture of one finger with complete recovery within a few weeks.	Up to £3,000
(r)	**Loss of Thumb**	£20,000 - £35,000
(s)	**Very Serious Injury to Thumb**	£15,000 - £30,000
(t)	Injury to thumb involving amputation of tip, nerve damage or fracture necessitating insertion of wires, and operative treatment leaving limb cold and ultra-sensitive, or leading to impairment of grip and loss of manual dexterity.	£10,000 - £20,000

(u) Moderate Thumb Injuries	£7,500 - £15,000
(v) Severe Dislocation of the Thumb	)
	) Up to £7,500
(w) Minor Thumb Injuries	)

(x) Cases of Vibration White Finger

(This is not an orthopaedic injury)

This is a particular form of Raynaud's phenomenon caused by prolonged exposure to vibration.

(i) Extensive blanching of most fingers with episodes in summer and winter of such severity as to necessitate changing occupation to avoid further exposure to vibration.	Up to £7,500 - £10,000
(ii) Blanching of one or more fingers with numbness. Usually occurring only in winter and causing slight interference with home and social activities.	£4,000 - £6,000
(iii) Blanching one or more fingertips, with or without tingling and numbness.	Up to £3,000

J. Work-related Upper Limb Disorders

This section covers a range of upper limb injury in the form of the following pathological conditions from finger to elbow.

(a) Tenosynovitis. Inflammation of synovial sheaths of tendons usually resolving with rest over a short period. Sometimes it leads to continuing symptoms of loss of grip and dexterity.

(b) De Quervain's tenosynovitis. A form of tenosynovitis, rarely bilateral, involving inflammation of the tendons of the thumb.

(c) Tenovaginitis stenovans. Otherwise trigger finger/thumb: thickening of tendons.

(d) Carpal tunnel syndrome. Constriction of the median nerve of the wrist or thickening of surrounding tissue, often relieved by decompression operation.

(e) Epicondylitis. Inflammation in the elbow joint: medial (golfer's elbow), lateral (tennis elbow).

The various levels of award below apply to each such condition. The following considerations affect the level of award regardless of the precise condition:

    (i)   Bilateral or one-sided

    (ii)   Level of symptoms (pain, swelling, tenderness, crepitus)

    (iii) Ability to work

    (iv) Capacity to avoid recurrence of symptoms

(a)	Continuing bilateral disability with surgery and loss of employment	£10,000 - £25,000
(b)	Continuing symptoms, but fluctuating and unilateral	£10,000 - £15,000
(c)	Symptoms resolving over two years	£5,000 - £7,500
(d)	Complete recovery within a short period	Up to £5,000

K. Leg Injuries

(a)	**Total Loss of Both Legs**	£150,000 - £250,000
(b)	**Below Knee Amputation of Both Legs**	£100,000 - £200,000
(c)	**Above Knee Amputation of One Leg**	£100,000 - £150,000
(d)	**Below Knee Amputation of One Leg**	£75,000 - £125,000

(e) Leg Injuries

(i)   There are some injuries which, although not involving amputation of the leg, are nevertheless so severe that the courts have awarded damages in the same region. Examples would be a degloving injury from knee to ankle, gross shortening of the leg, non-union of fractures and extensive bone grafting.   £50,000 - £125,000

(ii) Awards within this bracket will be made where the injuries leave permanent disability necessitating the use of crutches for the remainder of a person's life and very limited walking capacity; where multiple fractures have taken years to heal with resulting leg deformity and limitation of movement; or where arthrosis has developed in eg the knee joint and further surgical treatment is likely to be necessary.   £50,000 - £100,000

(iii) A claim may be brought within this bracket by reason of such factors as significant damage to a joint or ligaments causing instability, prolonged treatment or a lengthy period non-weight bearing, substantial and unsightly scarring, the likelihood of arthrodesis to the hip, the near certainty of arthritis setting in, the gross restriction of walking capacity and the need for hip replacement. A combination of such features will be necessary to justify such an award.

£40,000 - £75,000

(iv) This level of award still applies to relatively serious injuries, including severe, complicated or multiple fractures. The position of an award within this bracket will be influenced by the period of time off work and by the presence or risk of degenerative changes, imperfect union of fractures, muscle wasting, limited joint movements, instability of the knee, unsightly scarring and permanently increased vulnerability to damage.

£30,000 - £60,000

(v) Most awards that fall within this range comprise fractures where there has been incomplete recovery.

£17,500 - £30,000

Examples are:

A defective gait, a limp, impaired mobility, sensory loss, discomfort or an exacerbation of a pre-existing disability.

(vi) Simple fracture of femur, with no damage to articular surfaces.

£7,500 - £12,500

(vii) Simple fracture of the tibia or fibula with complete recovery will attract a figure towards the top of the bracket. Below that level will be a variety of different types of soft tissue injuries, lacerations, cuts, severe bruising or

contusions all of which will have recovered completely or almost completely, with any residual disability comprising scarring or being of a minor nature.	Up to £7,500

L. Knee Injuries

(a)	This bracket is appropriate to the serious knee injury where there has been disruption of the joints, gross ligamentous damage, lengthy treatment, considerable pain and loss of function and an arthrodesis has taken place or is inevitable.	£30,000 - £60,000
(b)	This applies where a leg fracture extends into the knee-joint causing pain which is constant, permanent, limits movement or impairs agility and renders the injured person prone to osteoarthritis and the risk of arthrodesis.	£25,000 - £50,000
(c)	The injuries justifying awards falling within this bracket are less serious than those in the higher bracket and/or result in less severe disability. There may be continuing symptoms by way of pain or discomfort and limitation of movement or instability and deformity with the risk of degenerative changes occurring in the long term, consequent upon ligamentous or meniscal injury, damage to the kneecap or muscular wasting.	£15,000 - £30,000
(d)	This bracket is appropriate to cases involving a torn cartilage or meniscus, dislocation, ligamentous damage and the like or injuries which accelerate symptoms from a pre-existing condition but which injuries additionally result in	

minor instability, wasting, weakness or other mild future disability	£15,000 - £20,000

(e) Awards in this bracket will be made in respect of injuries less serious than but similar to bracket (d) or in respect of lacerations, twisting or bruising injuries. Injuries resulting in continuous aching or discomfort or occasional pain will attract awards towards the upper end of the bracket.   Up to £10,000

M. Ankle Injuries

(a) Examples of injuries in this bracket include:

Transmalleolar fracture of the ankle with extensive soft tissue damage resulting in deformity and the risk that any future injury to the leg might necessitate a below knee amputation. Bilateral ankle fractures causing degeneration of the joints at the young age necessitating arthrodesis.   £30,000 - £60,000

(b) Awards in this bracket are justified where the ankle injury is severe necessitating an extensive period of treatment and/or lengthy period in plaster or with pins and plates inserted and where there is significant residual disability by way of ankle instability, severely limited ability to walk etc. The position within the bracket will, in part, be determined by, eg a failed arthrodesis, regular disturbance of sleep, unsightly operational scarring and any need to wear special footwear.   £25,000 - £50,000

(c) In this area fall the fractures, ligamentous tears and the like, giving rise to less serious disabilities such as difficulty walking over uneven ground, awkwardness on stairs, irritation from metal plates and residual scarring.

£12,500 - £30,000

(d) Less serious, minor or undisplaced fractures, sprains and ligamentous injuries. The position within the scale would be determined by whether or not a complete recovery has been made and if not whether there is any tendency for the ankle to give way, any scarring, aching or discomfort, or the possibility of later osteoarthritis.

Up to £12,500

N. Achilles Tendon

(a) Where there has been severance of the tendon and peroneus longus muscle giving rise to cramp, swelling and restricted ankle movement necessitating the cessation of active sports.

£15,000 - £30,000

(b) This figure is appropriate for an injury resulting in complete division of the tendon, followed by a successful repair operation but leaving residual weakness, a limitation of ankle movements, a limp and residual scarring with further improvement unlikely.

£12,500 - £25,000

(c) Complete division of the tendon but with no significant functional disability.

£7,500 - £15,000

(d) Ankle turned resulting in damage to tendon and feeling of being unsure of ankle support.

Up to £7,500

O. Foot Injuries

(a)	**Amputation of Both Feet**	£100,000 - £200,000
(b)	**Amputation of One Foot**	£75,000 - £125,000

(c) Serious foot injuries such as traumatic amputation of a forefoot when its effect was to exacerbate a pre-existing back problem and where there was a significant risk of the need for complete amputation. Similarly an injury resulting in the loss of a substantial portion of the heel and limited mobility.

£50,000 - £100,000

(d) This level of award is suitable for severe injuries, such as where there have been fractures to both heels or feet with substantially restricted mobility or considerable or permanent pain in both feet. This bracket is also suitable to unusually severe injuries to a single foot which have resulted in heel fusion, osteoporosis, ulceration or other disability preventing the wearing of ordinary shoes.

£40,000 - £75,000

(e) Towards the top end of this bracket would come the injury resulting in grievous burns to both feet requiring several operations but nevertheless leaving disfiguring scars and persisting irritation.

Lower in the bracket are those injuries which are less severe but nevertheless result in fusion of foot joints, continuing pain from traumatic arthritis, prolonged treatment and the future risk of osteoarthritis.

£20,000 - £50,000

(f) This bracket is appropriate for displaced metatarsal fractures resulting in permanent deformity and continuing symptoms.		
		£15,000 - £25,000
(g) This level of award applies to the relatively modest injuries such as metatarsal fractures, ruptured ligaments, puncture wounds and the like.		
		Up to £12,500

P. Toe Injuries

(a) Amputation of all Toes		£20,000 - £40,000
The position in the bracket will be determined by the extent of loss of the forefoot, and residual effects on mobility.		
(b) Amputation of Great Toe		£15,000 - £30,000
(c) This is the appropriate bracket for severe crush injuries, falling short of the need for amputation or necessitating only partial amputation. It also includes bursting wounds and injuries resulting in severe damage and in any event producing continuing significant symptoms.		
		£12,500 - £25,000

(d) This bracket will apply to serious fractures of the great toe or to crush and multiple fractures of any toes. There would have to be some permanent disability by way of discomfort, pain or sensitive scarring to justify an award within this bracket. A number of unsuccessful operations, stabbing pain, impaired gait and the like would place the award towards the top end of the bracket.   £7,500 - £20,000

(e) This level of award applies to modest injuries including relatively straightforward fractures or the exacerbation of a pre-existing degenerative condition.   Up to £7,500

7. FACIAL INJURIES

The assessment of general damages for facial injuries is an extremely difficult task, there being two elements which complicate the award.

First, while in most of the cases dealt with below the injuries described are skeletal, many of them will involve an element of disfigurement or at least cosmetic disability.

Secondly, in cases where there is a cosmetic element the courts have invariably drawn a distinction between the awards of damages to males and females, the latter attracting the higher awards.

The subject of burns is not dealt with separately because burns of any degree of severity tend to be so devastating as to be invariably at the upper ends of the brackets.

In the guidance which follows some effort has been made to distinguish these types of cases but the above considerations must always be borne in mind. Where there is a cosmetic element care must be taken to endeavour to remain broadly within the guidelines which are extracted from reported decisions wherein a subjective element was taken into account.

A. Skeletal Injuries

(a) Le Fort Fractures of frontal facial bones.	£15,000 - £30,000
(b) Multiple fractures of facial bones involving some facial deformity of a permanent nature.	£12,500 - £25,000

(c)   Fracture of Nose

(i)   Serious fractures requiring a number of operations and resulting in permanent damage to airways and/or facial deformity.   £10,000 - £20,000

(ii) Simple undisplaced with full recovery.   )
)
)
(iii) Displaced fracture requiring no more than manipulation.   ) Up to £5,000
)
(iv) Displaced where recovery complete but only after surgery.   )
)

(d)   Fractures of Cheek-Bones

(i)   Serious fractures requiring surgery but with lasting consequences such as paraesthesia in the cheeks or the lips or some element of disfigurement.   £10,000 - £20,000

(ii) Simple fracture of cheek-bones for which no surgery is required and a complete recovery is effected.   )
)
) Up to £7,500
(iii) Simple fracture of cheek-bones for which some reconstructive surgery is necessary but from which there is a complete recovery with no or only minimal cosmetic effects.   )
)

(e)   Fractures of Jaws

(i)   Very serious fractures followed by prolonged treatment and permanent consequences, including severe pain, restriction in eating, paraesthesia

and/or the risk of arthritis in the joints.		£15,000 - £35,000
(ii)	Serious fracture with permanent consequences such as difficulty in opening the mouth or with eating or where there is paraesthesia in the area of the jaw.	£10,000 - £20,000
(iii)	Simple fracture requiring immobilisation but from which recovery is complete.	£5,000 - £7,500

(f) Damage to Teeth

In these cases there will generally have been a course of dental treatment. The amounts awarded will vary as to the extent and discomfort of such treatment. Costs incurred to the date of trial will, of course, be special damage but it will often be necessary to award a capital sum in respect of the cost of future dental treatment.

(i)	Loss of or Serious Damage to Several Front Teeth	£5,000 - £15,000
(ii)	Loss of Two Front Teeth	Up to £8,000
(iii)	Loss of One Front Tooth	Up to £5,000
(iv)	Loss of or Damage to Back Teeth: per tooth	Up to £1,000

B. Facial Disfigurement

This is an almost impossible area for generalisation.

In this class of case the distinction between male and female and the subjective approach are of particular significance:

(a) Females

(i)	Very severe facial scarring in a relatively young girl (teens to early thirties) where the cosmetic effect is very disfiguring and the psychological reaction severe.	£50,000 - £150,000 It is recognised that there could be exceptional cases falling outside the bracket.
(ii)	Less severe scarring where the disfigurement is still substantial and where there is a significant psychological reaction.	£20,000 - £50,000
(iii)	Significant scarring where the worst effects have been or will be reduced by plastic surgery leaving some cosmetic disability and where the psychological reaction is not great or having been considerable at the outset has diminished to relatively minor proportions.	£15,000 - £50,000
(iv)	Some scarring but not of great significance, either because there is but one scar which can be camouflaged or because although there are a large number of very small scars the overall effect is to mar but not markedly to affect the appearance and where the reaction is no more than that of an ordinary sensitive young woman.	Up to £20,000

(b) Males

(i)	Particularly severe facial scars especially in males under 30, where there is permanent disfigurement even after plastic surgery and a	£40,000 - £125,000 There could be exceptional cases

	considerable element of psychological reaction.	falling outside the bracket.
(ii)	Severe facial scarring leaving moderate to severe permanent disfigurement.	£20,000 - £50,000
(iii)	Significant but not severe scars which will remain visible at conversational distances.	Up to £20,000
(iv)	Relatively minor scarring which is not particularly prominent except on close inspection.	Up to £10,000
(v)	Trivial scarring where the effect is minor only.	Up to £5,000

8. SCARRING TO OTHER PARTS OF THE BODY

This is an area in which it is not possible to offer much useful guidance. The principles are the same as those applied to cases of facial disfigurement and the brackets are broadly the same. It must be remembered that many of the physical injuries already described involve some element of disfigurement and that element is of course taken into account in suggesting the appropriate bracket. There of course remain some cases where the element of disfigurement is the predominant one in the assessment of damages. Where the scarring is not to the face or is not usually visible then the awards will tend to be lower than those for facial or readily visible disfigurement.

The effects of burns will normally be regarded as more serious since they tend to cause a greater degree of pain and to lead to greater disfigurement.

9. DAMAGE TO HAIR

(a) Damage to hair in consequence of permanent waving, tinting or the like, where the effects are tingling or "burning" of the scalp causing dry, brittle hair, which breaks off and/or falls out leading to distress, depression, embarrassment and loss of confidence, and inhibiting social life. In the more serious cases thinning continues and the prospects of regrowth are poor or there has been total loss of areas of hair and regrowth is slow.

(b) Less serious versions of the above where symptoms are fewer or only of a minor character; also, cases where the hair has been pulled out leaving bald patches. The level of the award will depend on the length of time taken before regrowth occurs.

) Up to £15,000

10. DERMATITIS

(a) Gross cases causing pain and discomfort, and likely to continue, affecting work severely.

£20,000 - £40,000

(b) Rash which covers other parts of body and lasts more than 3 years and may continue.

£12,500 - £25,000

(c) Primary Irritant rash on hands which clears up or is likely to clear in 2/3 years.

£5,000 - £12,500

(d) Allergic rash as above.

£5,000 - £15,000

(e) A rash which clears up in a matter of months.

Up to £5,000

INDEX

45